WE WERE HERE FIRST
THE NATIVE AMERICANS

THE
CREEK

Russell Roberts

PURPLE TOAD
PUBLISHING

WE WERE HERE FIRST
THE NATIVE AMERICANS

Printing 1 2 3 4 5 6 7 8 9

Publisher's Cataloging-in-Publication Data
Roberts, Russell.
   Creek / written by Russell Roberts.
      p. cm.
Includes bibliographic references, glossary, and index.
   ISBN 9781624693106
1. Creek Indians--Juvenile literature. 2. Indians of North America--Southern States. I. Series: We Were Here First: The Native Americans.
   E99.C9 2017
   976.1004
Library of Congress Control Number: 2016957218
eBook ISBN: 9781624693113

PUBLISHER'S NOTE: With special thanks to Dr. James King for taking the time to meet with Purple Toad Publishing's author and consultant, Wayne Wilson.

About Dr. James King: A Muscogee (Creek) Living Legend, Dr. James King is the College of the Muscogee Nation's Regents Director of Institutional Effectiveness. He has also served as President of the College of the Muscogee Nation. Read more about Dr. King at https://academics.nsuok.edu/isdc/AdvisoryBoard/DrJamesKing.aspx

Note: Today, many Creek refer to themselves as Muscogee. This accurately describes their language and culture. Since this book contains historical information, the term "Creek" is used, as it provides historical context.

CONTENTS

Even in modern times, the Creek and other Native Americans have had to stand up and fight to protect their homelands.

CHAPTER 1
A NEW BATTLE WITH AN OLD THEME

Everyone was tense. It was a new battle, with a very old and familiar theme.

On one side of the argument stood thousands of Native Americans from more than 200 tribes. Each one was determined to protect their land for their people. On the other side stood construction crews who were under orders to dig into that land as part of the 1,172-mile-long Dakota Access oil pipeline. This standoff was not part of a battle from long ago, however. Instead, it happened in autumn 2016 in North Dakota.

All of the Native Americans were there to say no, you cannot tear up and build on this land. It was only a half mile from the Standing Rock Sioux reservation. The Sioux worried that a possible oil leak could threaten the tribe's water supply. Others agreed. "The threat to water by an oil leak affects not just Native Americans, but every living being in this country," Cindy Yahola, a member of the Muscogee Creek Nation, told *People's World*.[1] In addition, tearing up the ground for construction would destroy tribal burial grounds and other sacred sites.

Protesters of the pipeline had their horses nose to nose with police officers. Finally, in December, 2016, officials chose not to approve the proposed pipeline route under Lake Oahe in North Dakota, marking a huge victory for the Native American tribes who stood against it.

The Creek were among the tribes who had signed up to support the Sioux. One of the Creek's National Council representatives, Mark Randolph, told a reporter, "I thought, how can we help them, how can we support them . . . because what happens to them eventually happens to us."[2]

The Creek gathered donations for the protesters. They also brought them a truck full of water, food, and other supplies. "We had water, we had money donations, we had toiletries, shampoo, hair brushes, everything from A to Z that you could camp with and help take care of yourself," said another Muscogee Creek Nation member, Rojer Johnson.[3]

The Muscogee/Creek Today

Supporting other tribes like the Sioux is one of the many ways the Muscogee/Creek show respect for their rich history. Today, the majority of Muscogee live in Oklahoma. They are known as the Oklahoma Creek Indians. Their capital is in the city of Okmulgee.

Traditions and ceremonial clothing are still important to the Poarch Band of Creek Indians.

About 2,340 Creeks currently live in Escambia County in southern Alabama. They are called the Poarch Band of Creek Indians. They have their own system of government and laws. According to Dr. James King, a member of the Muscogee Creek Nation and one of the developers of the group's tribal college, their government addresses any issues or problems that might arise among the people. Like the U.S. government, the tribal system has three branches (legislative, executive, and judicial). It also has a built-in system of checks and balances. "No one individual is making

decisions," explains King. "People may have differences of opinion, but there are methods to resolve those."[4]

The tribe keeps their legacy alive by holding powwows each year. They also hold Green Corn ceremonies. People come from all over the area to take part in these festivals. Visitors can also learn

Green corn stalks are used in ritual fires.

The log Council House that was built in 1868 burned down ten years later. It was replaced by a stone building, which was remodeled in the 1990s.

more about the tribe's history by visiting the Council House in downtown Okmulgee. Originally built in 1868, it was completely updated and remodeled during the 1990s. Today, it is a museum for the tribe's history. It has been listed as a National Historical Landmark since 1961.[5]

The remodeling of the museum cost more than $1 million. Most of the money was raised locally. Museum director Debbie Martin told a local news station that a fascinating surprise was found during the renovation. "In between the ceiling and the second floor we found an adze—a wood planing tool," she explained. "Someone laid it down and it stayed there for a hundred years. It was in perfect condition."[6]

The museum is full of many Muscogee treasures. Exhibits date as far back as prehistoric times and come up to current day. A library features hundreds of cemetery records, as well as photographs. A gift shop offers tribal sculptures, paintings, pottery, and clothing. As Martin puts it, "If you can't find it anywhere else, it's here."[7] The museum is an inviting way to remind some and introduce others to the rich history behind the Muscogee tribe.

A Creek Tale—or Tail

Black tail stripes and an eye mask are the quickest way to identify a raccoon (left).

A long time ago, Opossum was taking a walk through the woods just as the sun was going down. He spotted Raccoon and frowned. He had always been jealous of his friend's beautiful black-and-white ringed tail. "How did you get all of those pretty rings?" he finally asked Raccoon.

Raccoon reached back and stroked his long, fluffy tail with pride. "I wrapped bark around it here, here, and here," he replied. "Then I stuck my tail into the fire. The fur between the strips of bark turned black. The other areas remained white."

Opossum could not wait to try this. He gathered pieces of bark and wrapped them around his tail. Next, he built a huge fire and stuck his tail into it. Ouch! The bonfire was too big and too hot. All of the hair on Opossum's tail was burned off, leaving it bare. Opossum moaned and groaned. He hoped his fur would grow back. He waited, waited, and waited, but it never did.

Even today, every Opossum's tail is bare—and Raccoon laughs.

Cahokia was once a city covering more than five square miles and filled with thousands of people.

CHAPTER 2
THE MISSISSIPPI CULTURE

When the first Spanish explorers came to the southeastern part of North America in the early 1500s, they ran into a group of natives called the Mississippi Culture. They were fascinating to the visitors! The Mississippi Culture began around 700 CE in the central Mississippi River Valley. Over the next 200 years, the group spread across the southeast. The largest town was Cahokia. Historians believe as many as 20,000 people lived there.[1]

The people grew their food, planting maize (corn), beans, and other crops. To make sure the crops grew well, the people lived near rivers. There, the soil was fertile and water was plentiful. They also built large mounds of earth as high as 50 feet. These were used as the foundations for religious temples and homes. Some of these huge mounds can still be seen today.

By the middle of the fourteenth century, the Mississippi Culture began to fade. By 1539, when Spanish explorer Hernando de Soto and his army of hundreds arrived on Florida's west coast, few of them were left. De Soto had come to the land in search of gold and treasure. He and his men terrorized the native people. They captured men and women

De Soto, like so many other foreign explorers, surveyed new lands. He immediately began making unreasonable demands of the people who lived there.

and made them slaves. They demanded food. They held people hostage to make sure their demands were met. If the explorers met any resistance, they attacked, killing many of the Native Americans.

The frightened natives fled their villages. Fields and crops fell into ruin. When De Soto failed to find his riches, he moved on, leaving behind smallpox and plague. Natives died by the thousands. The diseases may have killed 90 percent of the entire native population.[2]

Becoming the Creek

During the late 1700s, more and more English colonists moved to the southeast. It was the traders who first started calling the Native Americans there "Creek," since many of the natives lived near Ochese Creek (now Ocmulgee River in Georgia). Soon, the English referred to all natives in the Georgia and Alabama areas as Creek.

The Creeks lived in two separate areas 100 miles apart, so they rarely saw each other. The Upper Creeks lived along the Coosa and Tallapoosa rivers in Alabama. The Lower Creeks settled near the Atlantic and Gulf coasts, as well as near Georgia's Chattahoochee and Flint Rivers.

The English traders wanted deerskins from the Creeks. The market for these skins was growing, and thousands were needed in order to make leather goods. In exchange for these skins, the Creeks were given guns, cloth, ammunition, beads, and metal tools.

Trading various types of animal skins for other goods was one way the Creek got the items they needed to hunt.

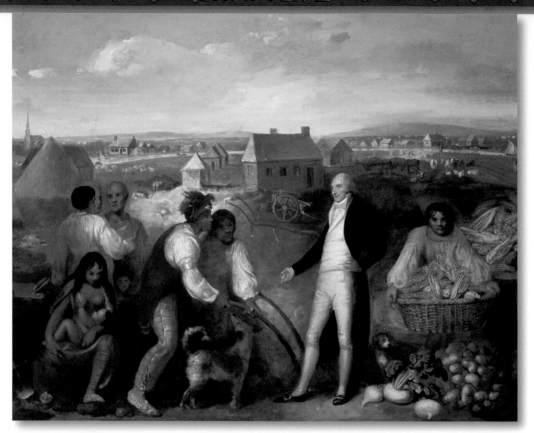

In this painting, plantation owner Benjamin Hawking teaches Creek slaves how to farm like Europeans, including how to use a plow.

At the same time, Creeks began trading slaves. English traders wanted to sell these slaves to plantation owners. The Creeks only had a few captives to trade, so they began attacking neighboring tribes and Spanish missions in order to take prisoners. England was pleased! Not only did they get more slaves, but it kept the natives battling each other instead of them. They even provided the Creek with the weapons they needed. It was not long before the tribe had become one of the most powerful groups in the Southeast.

The Yamasee War

The arrangement did not last forever, however. Some of the Creeks, including a group called the Yamasee, were becoming more and more unhappy with the English colonists. If any natives traded for goods and could not meet their debts, the traders would take them as slaves. Unrest grew.

In April 1715, natives from many different nations throughout the southeast began battling the colonists. It was one of the most powerful native uprisings in American history. Nearly 10 percent of the white population of South Carolina was killed.[3] Despite this, by 1717, the war was over. The colonists won, but the war ended the native slave trade.

The Yamasee War was one of the bloodiest wars in American history. Native tribes killed more than 400 traders, settlers, and colonists, plus set fire to plantations in South Carolina.

The Creek made the most of the competition between the European countries, gathering as many goods as they could.

Without an active slave trade, the Creek went back to hunting deer and trading the animal skins for goods they needed. At this time, the French and English were competing to see who could be the most powerful in North America. France knew one way to do this was to win over the Native Americans and get their support. They began giving the tribes tools, weapons, and cloth. England and Spain were not about to fall behind, so they started matching each of these gifts. The Creek leaders played the European countries off each other so that they could get more goods.

Then everything changed.

The Creek Confederacy

General James Oglethorpe meets with the Creeks while planning his own settlement in Georgia. He and other Europeans had no idea how large the Creek population was.

When the first Europeans came to America, they thought the Creeks were a single tribe. Actually, the Creeks were a union of many tribes. They included the Muscogee, Yuchi, Apalachicola, Alabama, and Hitchiti. By the early 1700s, these tribes had joined together to form the Creek Confederacy. Towns in the confederacy might band together for festivals, tribal meetings, and trade. However, each town was independent and acted in its own interests.

Native Americans of many tribes enjoyed playing the fast and physical game of stickball. While it was often done for fun, it was also played to determine the winner of an argument.

CHAPTER 3
WELCOME TO
THE *TALWA*

Anyone stepping back into time to visit a Creek village, or *talwa*, would see a large open space known as the town or central square. During the summer, meetings were held outside in the square. In the winter, they were held inside a special council building. Another section of the square was used for dancing during ceremonies or for playing stickball, a game much like today's lacrosse. Stickball was not just a fun game to play. It also helped settle arguments between towns and clans.

Surrounding the central square were family homes. The houses were usually made of mud and straw. Animal hides were put on the walls to keep out the wind and rain. A single Creek family could have as many as four properties: a summer house, a winter house, a building for entertaining guests, and a storehouse for keeping various goods and animal hides.

The Creek had more than 50 villages, and each one was run by a *miko*, or chief. A number of other sub-chiefs and counselors helped him make decisions about everything from when to hold a town meeting or arrange a festival to who should win in a dispute or if it was time to declare war.

Creek women and children spent hours looking through the forests for any edible herbs, berries, or nuts to add to their daily menu.

Each village had a common field that served everyone. Within the field, each family had a plot. The Creek grew corn, squash, sweet potatoes, beans, and pumpkins. The women were in charge of the farming, so they planted and harvested, as well as gathered roots, berries, and herbs. While the women were working in the fields, the men were hunting for meat and animal skins, or they were fishing. They used spears and arrows to catch smaller fish. Lassoes made from strong vines were used to catch larger ones.

Within the Clans

Each of the Creek villages was made up of clans. The Creek had a total of more than 40 clans. Each one had a special name such as Deer, Corn, Beaver, or Wind. A child became a member of the same clan as his or her mother. Children were related to the clan of their mother, not of their father. A Creek boy was taught life

Creek chief Tomochichi and his nephew, Toonahawi

skills by his uncles (his mother's brothers). A Creek girl was taught life skills by her mother.

A young Creek person could not marry someone from the same clan. When a man wanted to marry a woman, he gave her a gift. If she accepted it, the man moved in with her until the wedding. After the two were married, he moved into the family compound of his wife. When a Creek woman became pregnant, she was particularly careful about what she ate. The Creeks believed that a bite of rabbit could make the child's eyes too large. A meal with squirrel could make a child too nervous. Bear would give bad temper. On the other hand, venison (deer meat) would make the child strong.

Creek children were treasures that were watched carefully and taught well how to survive.

Of Gods and Worlds

The Creek's main god was known as the Master of Breath. He was responsible for all good things in life. He made sure the waters were pure, the hunt was productive, and the corn was plentiful. He was the creator of both Brother Moon and Sister Sun. He created the four directions (north, south, east, and west) that held up the world.

The Creek believed in three worlds: this world, the Upper World, and the Lower World. This world was where people, animals, and plants lived. It floated on a pool of water and was covered by a bowl-shaped sky chamber of solid rock. At each dawn and dusk, the chamber rose so that the sun and moon could slip underneath it.

A carving of a Falcon dancer found at a dig site shows images of Creek priests and warriors.

The mysterious sun and moon meant a great deal to the Creek. They wore special jewelry with these images to show their respect.

The Upper World was where the sun, moon, and other beings existed. It was also the source of order, perfection, and wisdom. The Creek people called upon some of these elements by wearing special jewelry with images of the sun or moon.

The Lower World was a place of ghosts, monsters, and madness. It was where dangerous spirit creatures like the Tie-Snake lived. The Tie-Snake looked like a giant dragon with antlers. Its scales were said to have strong powers.[1]

Hvuse was the sun god of the Muscogee. He was considered to be the father of the corn goddess. The Creek considered fire to be the sun put on Earth.

The Creek believed it was very important to keep the Upper and Lower Worlds separate. Fire, which belonged to the Upper World, was never put out with water, as water was from the Lower World. The people used sand instead.

The natives had no way of knowing that soon their worlds would collide. Creek life would never be the same again.

Celebration Time

Each summer the Creek people celebrated the ripening of the corn with the Green Corn Dance. This festival lasted for more than a week, and it was a time for everyone to start over. All grudges were forgotten. All crimes (except for the most serious) were forgiven. The people swam in nearby creeks to wipe away the old and welcome in the new. During this time, the village's council fire, which stayed lit all year round, was put out. A new fire was started to signal all new beginnings. In homes throughout the village, the women put out their fires and lit new ones from the new council fire.

The corn goddess was called Uvce. As the daughter of the sun god, it was her job to create corn, beans, and wormseed, a powerful medicine.

The French and Indian War was fought mainly between the colonies of Great Britain and New France, with both sides aided by forces from Europe as well as Native American allies.

CHAPTER 4
CHOOSING SIDES

For years, the Creeks and other tribes hunted deer to meet the European demand for animal skins. With more and more tribes hunting, the forests soon had fewer and fewer deer. By the late 1700s, Creek hunters were finding "deer and bear to be scarce."[1] These men had to travel farther and farther from their homes. They were gone for longer periods of time, and soon life in the villages began to change. Men were not around to teach their nephews important skills. Tribal decisions were postponed—or never made. As hunters from the different tribes began to compete to find deer, they began seeing each other as enemies. Fights broke out between the Creeks and the Choctaws.

In 1763, the British won the French and Indian War. British colonists flooded into the lands where the Creek had always lived. The colonists began to demand more and more land. Suddenly, Creek villages were surrounded by English settlers and troops.

The problems did not stop there. Trading between the Creeks and the British was tense. Over the years, the Creeks

The Creeks met many times to try to solve their trading problems. They agreed they had to sell some land to pay their debts.

had grown dependent upon trading to get cloth, weapons, and tools. At the same time, England's demand for deerskins was fading. The Native Americans did not have anything else to trade, so they often went into debt getting the goods they wanted. The traders took advantage of this, charging outrageously high prices for their items. Some even deliberately got the Creek traders drunk so that they were easier to cheat.

The Creeks tried to fix these trade problems. From 1763 to 1773, they held six trade conferences with the British. It did not help the situation. The Creek still owed the traders money, and the colonists still wanted more land. In the end, the Creek wound up selling land in Georgia and Florida to Great Britain.

Time for War

Tension between the new colonists and the English government grew in the early 1770s. Finally the American Revolutionary War began, and the Creeks found themselves right in the middle. Both sides wanted the natives to fight for them. The Creeks did not want to interrupt the flow of English goods by supporting the colonists. They also did not want to be attacked by either side and have their homes burned and their crops destroyed, as had happened to the Cherokee.

When the Revolution ended in 1783, the colonists had won. The Creeks had a lot of changes to adjust to now that they were officially part of the United States. The English were gone, and the Americans were in charge. Also, because of the Treaty of Paris, the colonists had been given additional

When British General Charles Cornwallis surrendered, it ended the Revolutionary War for the colonists. It also started more trouble for most Native Americans.

Benjamin West's painting from the 1783 Treaty of Paris shows Americans John Jay, John Adams, Benjamin Franklin, Henry Laurens, and William Temple Franklin. The British delegates refused to pose for the painting.

territory that had belonged to the Creeks. The Creeks were shocked. How could their land have been given by England to the Americans? How could this new country claim land that was not theirs?

A Creek chief named Alexander McGillivray strongly disagreed with the land transfer. Born in 1750 near present-day Montgomery, Alabama, his father was a Scottish trader and his mother was a Creek from the Wind Clan. McGillivray had a European-style education, but he also took part in Creek life and rituals. He was comfortable in both worlds. Abigail Adams, wife of vice president John Adams, called the man "grave and solid, intelligent and much of a gentleman."[2]

McGillivray wanted to protect Creek lands. He stated, "As we were not partys [to the Treaty of Paris], so we are determined to pay no attention to the Manner in which the British Negotiators . . . Ceded [the land] to the States of America."[3]

The chief wanted to unite all Creek towns under one central government. This idea was not popular with all of the Creek villages. Instead of uniting them, it split the Creek Nation into two sides.

McGillivray forged the 1784 Treaty of Pensacola with Spain. This treaty recognized the Creeks as an independent nation. The Creeks were given weapons and other goods and agreed to act as a

Alexander McGillivray

George Washington was the country's first president.

boundary between the U.S. and Florida. This would prevent Georgians from entering Spanish territory. It also made McGillivray a very powerful man politically.

At the same time, the chiefs in other Creek villages did not like the idea of a central Creek government. They signed different treaties that promised Georgia additional land. With the Creeks divided, the tribe was in trouble. Finally, the newly appointed President George Washington stepped in to help them find an answer. In 1790,

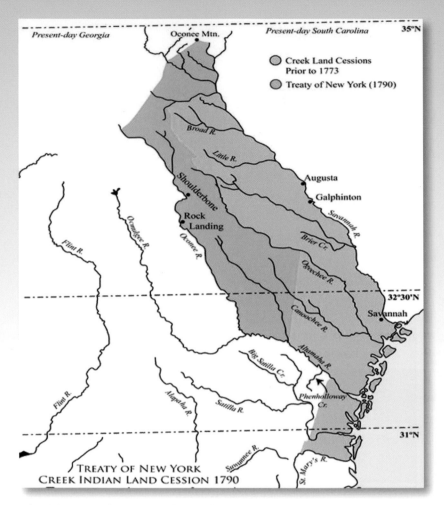

Present-day Georgia   Oconee Mtn.   Present-day South Carolina   35°N

○ Creek Land Cessions
Prior to 1773

○ Treaty of New York (1790)

Broad R.

Little R.

Shoulderbone

Augusta

Galphinton

Savannah R.

Rock
Landing

Brier Cr.

Ogeechee R.

Ocmulgee R.

Oconee R.

Flint R.

32°30'N

Savannah

Camoochee R.

Big Satilla Cr.

Altamaha R.

Flint R.

Alapaha R.

Satilla R.

Phenholloway
Cr.

31°N

TREATY OF NEW YORK
CREEK INDIAN LAND CESSION 1790

Suwannee R.

St. Mary's R.

**The Treaty of New York made it clear what land belonged
to the Creek—and what did not.**

McGillivray signed the Treaty of New York. It recognized the Creeks as an
independent nation, approved trade relations between the two sides, gave
the Creeks an annual payment, and promised to honor the boundaries of
the Creek nation. Creeks were placed under federal law. They sold the United
States three million acres of their land.

McGillivray's goal of uniting the Creeks seemed possible, but he died in
1793. His death left the Creeks lacking strong leadership just when they
needed it most.

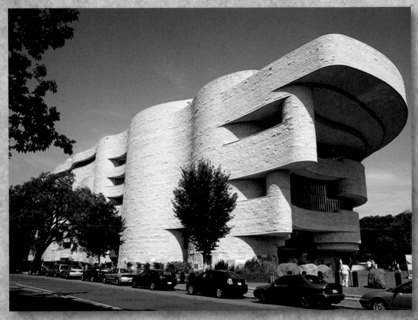

Museum of the American Indian

In March 2015, a group of Muscogee Native Americans traveled to Washington, D.C., from Oklahoma. The delegates wanted to honor the 1790 Treaty of New York. It included ceremonial leaders, plus the descendants of the Creeks who originally signed the treaty.

The National Museum of the American Indian created an exhibit called *Nation to Nation: Treaties between the United States and American Indian Nations*. Creek Nation Director Justin Giles told *Indian Country Today*, "This is a historic moment recognizing the relationship we've had with the U.S. for a number of centuries. The 1790 Treaty of New York is a living testament of what our ancestors accomplished, endured and negotiated for the well-being of the Muscogee (Creek) people and the Mvskoke way of life. . . . The issues of the treaty regarding land, boundaries, and friendship between the U.S. and the Muscogee (Creek) people continue to be an issue to this day."[4]

Tenskwatawa was named Lalawethika, or the Rattle, as a child. Later, his name was changed to mean the Prophet. He believed the Master of Life told him that all Native Americans must stop practicing white customs and using their goods.

CHAPTER 5
THE
RED STICK
WAR

Once more, life changed for the Creek after the Treaty of New York. The U.S. government decided it was time to "civilize" the Creek and other Native American tribes. The natives were pushed to become farmers, not hunters or warriors. A national Creek police force was established. These changes wreaked havoc in Creek life. Traditionally women had been the farmers, and now men were told it was their responsibility. Women were told to stay home with the children.

Many Creeks had little choice but to try farming if they wanted to avoid poverty. They attempted to adopt white ways so that the Americans would let them remain on their land. The natives of the Upper and Lower Creek did not agree on how much to change their lifestyles. This led to even greater divisions between the Creeks.

The Creeks were desperate to find a solution. In 1810, they found an answer in Shawnee brothers Tecumseh and Tenskwatawa, also known as the Prophet. Tenskwatawa had visions. He said that if Indians would reject the Americans and their teachings and return to traditional ways, they would be rewarded. The Americans would be expelled from their lands and all would return to normal.

Tecumseh

Tecumseh was a Shawnee war chief who adopted McGillivray's idea of a unified Indian nation. He traveled throughout the southeast preaching his message of unity and resistance. "[Do] not work, destroy the wheels and looms, throw away your ploughs, and every thing used by the Americans," he stated.[1] By spring 1813, the Upper and Lower Creek were fighting. A few months later, Americans got involved. At Alabama's Fort Sims, natives killed or captured 500 white settlers, militia, and Creeks. The Fort Sims Massacre panicked settlers. They demanded government action. Tennessee, Georgia, and Mississippi sent militia after the Red Sticks, or Upper Creek. For months, the two sides battled. On March 27, 1814, they found themselves at Horseshoe Bend.

Battle!

At 10:30 on this March morning, someone shouted, "Fire!" Two cannons erupted with a roar, aiming at a wall of logs before them. The cannonballs slammed into the stacked logs. Crouched behind them were about one thousand Creeks known as Red Sticks. Sharp chunks of wood hurtled through the air. A thick cloud of smoke settled over everything. It was absolute chaos.

After two hours, Tennessee Militia Major General Andrew Jackson ordered a bayonet charge. The Red Sticks were attacked from the front and the rear. Although their situation was hopeless, the Red Sticks kept fighting. Ultimately 800 of them were killed. The rest fled to Florida to join the Seminoles.

It was this battle and the Treaty of Fort Jackson that ended the Creek War. It also punished the Creek for fighting against Americans. The U.S. took 23 million acres of Creek land in southern Georgia and central Alabama. One historian called the Fort Jackson treaty "among the most punitive and destructive . . . in American-Indian affairs."[2]

The Creek War came to an end at the Battle of Horseshoe Bend.

After the Treaty

Settlers poured into the newly obtained lands. Food became scarce for the Creek. The Creek attempted to hold on to what territory they had left. In 1818, the Creek National Council announced that no more land could be sold—under penalty of death. This decision did not stop settlers from demanding more land, however. In 1821, Creek chief William McIntosh sold half of the Creek's land in Georgia in exchange for 1,000 acres of land in Indian Springs. In 1825, he sold that land as well. True to their word, the Creek National Council sentenced him to death, and he was killed.

The Trail of Tears was a terrible journey for every Native American who was forced to take it. Many did not survive the long, cold trip.

In 1830, Congress passed the Indian Removal Act. The act required the Creek, along with the Choctaw, Cherokee, Chickasaw, and Seminole, to move west of the Mississippi River. Pushed off their land, 20,000 Creek were forced to walk the Trail of Tears. Hungry and cold, one in ten Creek died on the miserable journey. Arriving in the west, the tribe faced more hardships. The new territory was completely unfamiliar. It was hard to start a new life in a place so different from the one they had known.

When the American Civil War began in 1861, both the Union and the Confederacy wanted the Creek on their side. Some Creeks chose the North and some the South. When the Union won the war, the U.S. government once again punished the Creek for fighting on both sides. The Creek had to give up half of their land in Oklahoma.

Despite their losses, the Creek knew that they were in this land first. Centuries before the Europeans arrived, they had homes, families, and a culture. They suffered much, but they endured and continued. Today most live in Oklahoma and Alabama. They are still proud of their heritage and eager to keep honoring their traditions.

Preserving the Past, Cultivating Futures

The College of the Muscogee Nation

Located in Okmulgee, Oklahoma, is the College of the Muscogee Nation. It was established in 2004 and covers 25 acres. This tribal college features two- and three-year degrees in unique classes not available at traditional colleges. They include Gaming, Tribal Services, Police Science, and Native American Studies. They also offer classes in Mvskoke Language, Native American History, Tribal Government, and Indian land issues. The college states that it is dedicated to five main values:

- Respect/Vrakkeuckv
- Integrity/Fvtcetv
- Reponsibility/Mecvlke
- Humility/Eyasketv
- Wisdom/Hoporenkv[3]

Locations: Alabama, Oklahoma, Georgia

Original Region: Southeast

Land area: 408,404 acres

Traditional name: Isti or Istichata

Population: 38,863 (2013)

The Creek Today: There are two main Creek groups today: the Poarch Band of Creek Indians in Alabama and the Oklahoma Creek Indians.

Favorite Food: Their staple food was corn.

The Origin of Their Name: The Creek tribe was said to be named after Ochese Creek near present-day Macon, Georgia.

Communities: The Creek built large towns, each with its own government. Each town included a community square. Some squares had a temple, and rectangular houses were built around the square.

Roots of the Creek: They originally migrated from Mexico.

700 CE	The Mississippi culture arises with farming and the growing of maize.
1539	Spanish explorer Hernando De Soto arrives in the Southeast.
1542	European diseases (smallpox, measles, and influenza) are introduced to the native people. They suffer an enormously high death rate. The survivors and their descendants regroup, leading to the rise of the Creek Confederacy.
1702	The Creeks ally with the British colonies in the Apalachee Wars. They raid Spanish Apalachee missions.
1715–1717	The Yamasee War ends the native slave trade.
1733	The Creeks trade with the Europeans. This and other close contact establishes strong cultural ties.
1763	The British win the French and Indian War, and colonists flock to Creek territory.
1775	The Creeks support the British in the American Revolutionary War.
1783	The colonists win the American Revolution. The State of Georgia begins its forceful expansion into Creek territory.
1790	The Treaty of New York is signed. It recognizes the Creeks as an independent nation. The Creeks sell three million acres of land to the United States.
1796	The U.S. government starts a program to "civilize" the Creek and other tribes.
1813–1814	The continued arrival of white settlers on Creek land provokes the Creek Wars.
1821 & 1825	Two treaties are signed, each called the Treaty of Indian Springs. They are negotiated by Creek leader William McIntosh. The treaties promise millions of acres of Creek land to Alabama.
1830	The Indian Removal Act is signed by President Andrew Jackson. It declares that all Native American tribes living in the Southeast must move west of the Mississippi River.
1832	The Treaty of Washington is signed. It surrenders to the United States all Creek land that is east of the Mississippi River.
1834	The Creek march to their new land west of the Mississippi River. The walk is so brutal for all the people who go that it becomes known as the Trail of Tears.
1865	After the Civil War, the Creek are forced to give up half their land in Oklahoma.
1867	The Muscogee Creek adopt a new constitution.
1907	Oklahoma becomes the 46th state. The Creek nation is divided into 8 counties.
1968	The Indian Civil Rights Act restores the right to hold popular elections among Native American tribes.
1970	The federal government permits the Creek Nation to elect its own principal chief.
1976	The success of the *Harjo v. Kleppe* lawsuit begins a new era for the Muscogee Creek Indian Nation. They rewrite the constitution and once again become self-governing.
2004	The College of the Muscogee Nation is founded. This public American Indian College is located in Okmulgee, Oklahoma, the capital of the Muscogee Nation.
2015	A Creek delegation travels to Washington, D.C., to honor the 1790 Treaty of New York.
2016	The Creek support the Standing Rock Sioux's protest of the Dakota Access Pipeline.

Chapter 1

1. Bender, Albert. "Tennessee Powwow Applauds Standing Rock Sioux Pipeline Opposition." *People's World*, September 28, 2016.

2. Caranzo, Honey. "MCN Shows Support for Standing Rock." *MVSkokeMedia*.com, September 14, 2016.

3. Mummolo, Burt. "Support for Standing Rock Sioux." Tulsa ABC, September 6, 2016.

4. King, Dr. James, interview with consultant, September 27, 2016.

5. "Muscogee (Creek) Nation Council House." *Muscogee (Creek) Nation*, May 2014.

6. Austerman, Lisa. "Creek Indian Museum an Okmulgee Treasure." *NewsOK*, October 25, 1998.

7. Ibid.

8. *American Folklore*. "Why Opossum Has a Bare Tail." Retold by S. E. Schlosser.

Chapter 2

1. Chickasaw TV. "Cahokia: The Largest Mississippian Archaeological Site on the North American Continent." Ancient Origins.net, September 25, 2014.

2. Jones, David S. "Epidemics in Indian Country." *American History*, December 2014.

3. Rose, Christina. "Native History: Yamasee War Ends Native Slave Trade, Upcoming Conference." *Indian Country Today*, March 25, 2015.

Chapter 3.

1. Grantham, Bill. *Creation Myths and Legends of the Creek Indians* (Gainesville: University Press of Florida, 2002), p. 25.

Chapter 4

1. Martin, Joel W. *Sacred Revolt* (Boston: Beacon Press, 1991), p. 67.

2. Tebbel, John, and Keith Jennison. *The American Indian Wars* (New York: Bonanza Books, 1960), p. 132.

3. Hudson, Angela Pulley. *Creek Paths and Federal Roads* (Chapel Hill: The University of North Carolina Press, 2010), p. 28.

4. Muscogee (Creek) Nation, "Muscogee Delegation Will Head to D.C. for 1790 Treaty of New York Display." *Indian Country Today*, March 15, 2015.

Chapter 5

1. Waselkov, Gregory A. *A Conquering Spirit* (Tuscaloosa: The University of Alabama Press, 2006), p. 73.

2. Hudson, Angela Pulley. *Creek Paths and Federal Roads* (Chapel Hill: The University of North Carolina Press, 2010), p. 117.

3. "Student Handbook." College of the Muscogee Nation, p. 2.

Books

Dwyer, Helen, and Amy Stone. *Creek History and Culture*. New York: Gareth Stevens Publishing, 2011.

KidCaps. *The Trail of Tears: A History Just for Kids!* CreateSpace Independent Publishing Platform, 2012.

Lant, Karla. *Andrew Jackson: A Controversial President*. Create Space Independent Publishing Platform, 2016.

Smith-Llera, Danielle. *The Creek: The Past and Present of the Muscogee (American Indian Life)*. North Mankato, MN: Capstone Press, 2016.

Tieck, Sarah, *Creek*. Edina, MN: Big Buddy Books, 2015.

Waterby, Ralph, *Muscogee (Creek) (Spotlight on Native Americans)*. New York: PowerKids Press, 2015.

On the Internet

The Lower Muscogee Creek Tribe Tama Tribal Town
http://lowerMuscogeetribe.com/home.html

The Muscogee (Creek) Nation
http://www.mcn-nsn.gov/

Native American Indian Facts: Creek Indian Facts
http://native-american-indian-facts.com/Southeast-American-Indian-Facts/Creek-Indians-Facts.shtml

Native American Legends: The Muscogee (Creek) Nation
http://www.legendsofamerica.com/na-creek.html

Native Languages of the Americas: Creek Indian Fact Sheet
http://www.bigorrin.org/creek_kids.htm

Native Languages of the Americas: Muscogee Culture and History
http://www.native-languages.org/Muscogee_culture.htm

Works Consulted

This book is based on consultant Wayne Wilson's interview with Dr. James King on September 27, 2016, and on the following sources:

American Folklore. "Why Opossum Has a Bare Tail." Retold by S. E. Schlosser. September 2010. http://americanfolklore.net/folklore/2010/09/why_opossum_has_a_bare_tail.html

Austerman, Lisa. "Creek Indian Museum an Okmulgee Treasure." *NewsOK*, October 25, 1998. http://newsok.com/article/2630747

Bender, Albert. "Tennessee Powwow Applauds Standing Rock Sioux Pipeline Opposition." *People's World*, September 28, 2016. http://www.peoplesworld.org/article/tenn-powwow-applauds-standing-rock-sioux-pipeline-opposition/

Caranzo, Honey. "MCN Shows Support for Standing Rock." *MVSkokeMedia.com*, September 14, 2016. http://mvskokemedia.com/mcn-shows-support-for-standing-rock/

Chickasaw TV. "Cahokia: The Largest Mississippian Archaeological Site on the North American Continent." *Ancient Origins*, September 25, 2014. http://www.ancient-origins.net/ancient-places-americas/cahokia-largest-mississippian-archaeological-site-north-america-1020500

College of the Muscogee Nation. http://www.mvsktc.org

Corkran, David H. *The Creek Frontier 1540–1783.* Norman: University of Oklahoma Press, 1967.

Grantham, Bill. *Creation Myths and Legends of the Creek Indians.* Gainesville: University Press of Florida, 2002.

Heidler, David S., and Jeanne T. Heidler. *Old Hickory's War.* Mechanicsburg, PA: Stackpole Books, 1996.

Hudson, Angela Pulley. *Creek Paths and Federal Roads.* Chapel Hill: The University of North Carolina Press, 2010.

Jones, David S. "Epidemics in Indian Country." *American History*, December 2014. http://americanhistory.oxfordre.com/view/10.1093/acrefore/9780199329175.001.0001/acrefore-9780199329175-e-27

Martin, Joel W. *Sacred Revolt*. Boston: Beacon Press, 1991.

Mummolo, Burt. "Support for Standing Rock Sioux." *Tulsa ABC*, September 6, 2016. http://ktul.com/news/local/support-for-standing-rock-sioux

"Muscogee (Creek) Nation Council House." *Muscogee (Creek) Nation*, May 2014. http://creekculturalcenter.com/2014/05/muscogee-creek-nation-council-house/

Muscogee (Creek) Nation, "Muscogee Delegation Will Head to D.C. for 1790 Treaty of New York Display." *Indian Country Today*, March 15, 2015. http://indiancountrytoday medianetwork.com/2015/03/15/muscogee-delegation-will-head-dc-1790-treaty-new-york-display-159569

Ohio History Central. "Tenskwatawa." http://www.ohiohistorycentral.org/w/Tenskwatawa

Piker, Joshua. *Okfuskee: A Creek Indian Town in Colonial America*. Cambridge, Mass.: Harvard University Press, 2004.

Rose, Christina. "Native History: Yamasee War Ends Native Slave Trade, Upcoming Conference." *Indian Country Today*, March 25, 2015. http://indiancountrytodaymedianetwork.com/2015/03/25/native-history-yamasee-war-ends-native-slave-trade-upcoming-conference-159745

Tebbel, John, and Keith Jennison. *The American Indian Wars*. New York: Bonanza Books, 1960.

Waselkov, Gregory A. *A Conquering Spirit*. Tuscaloosa: The University of Alabama Press, 2006.

adze (ADZ)—A Native American tool used since ancient times to plane wood.

chaos (KAY-os)—Great disorder or confusion.

confederacy (kun-FED-er-uh-see)—A group of people, countries, or organizations that join together in some type of activity or effort.

delegate (DEL-ih-git)—A person chosen to make important decisions on behalf of a larger group of people.

havoc (HAV-uk)—Confusion; disorder.

humility (hyoo-MIL-ih-tee)—The quality or state of being humble, of not thinking you are better than other people.

influence (IN-floo-untz)—The ability to produce change in others.

integrity (in-TEG-rih-tee)—Having strong values or morals.

powwow (POW-wow)—A Native American ceremony that usually includes dancing.

punitive (PYOO-nih-tiv)—Meant to punish someone or something.

Trail of Tears—The long march that tens of thousands of Native Americans were forced to make in the 1830s. The U.S. government forced them to move from the southeastern United States to lands west of the Mississippi River. The walk was over one thousand miles long. Thousands of Native Americans perished on the journey.

MEET THE
AUTHOR

Russell Roberts has researched, written, and published numerous books for both children and adults. Among his books for adults are *Down the Jersey Shore, Historical Photos of New Jersey,* and *Ten Days to A Sharper Memory.* He has written over 50 nonfiction books for children. Roberts often speaks on the subjects of his books before various groups and organizations. He lives in New Jersey.